SURVIVING A

TORNADO IN

OAKLAND CA

PT.1

TAJANEE FORD-WHELAN

TABLE OF CONTENTS

INTRODUCTION

Surviving a Tornado in Oakland, CA PT.1 is about my life, struggles, and triumphs. It is my testimony, perspective, and truth that I would like to share with all of you. I hope you take away some valuable lessons from my story, decisions, and mistakes. I hope you find light within the darkness, courage when you feel fear, and peace in the midst of chaos.

I believe childhood is the most critical part of our development. Our childhood experiences can have a profound impact on us throughout our lives. My family taught me many things. Some bad and some good. They taught me the same things they were taught by generations before them.

I was an innocent child who had been hurt mentally, emotionally, and physically. I learned negative behaviors and traits and grew up making poor decisions and mistakes. I was a victim and I turned into a villain.

I let my thoughts and emotions spin out of control. I became so consumed with negativity and darkness. I blamed others for everything wrong.

I began to have suicidal thoughts and I tried to kill myself on multiple occasions. I thought ending my life would be the best way to end my pain and suffering, but I was wrong.

We all make bad decisions and mistakes, but we can learn from them and move forward in a positive way. It is possible to change. It is possible to forgive ourselves and others. It is possible to forgive our trespassers. It is hard, but it is possible.

We can make it out of the darkness. We can see the light again, and we can be a light that shines upon others. Just Believe in God and Believe in yourself, Have Faith that everything will work out, and Manifest your dreams and goals.

I apologize to everyone I've hurt. I made some terrible decisions, and you all did not deserve the pain I caused. Please forgive me for the things I said and did wrong.

DEDICATION

I dedicate PT.1 to

my family and friends,

to my ancestors and grandparents,

to my aunts and uncles,

to my cousins, sisters, and brothers,

to my father,

but especially to my mother.

Thank you for

life, lessons, love, and support.

Thank you for raising me

to the best of your ability.

I know you did the best you could

with what you had

and with what you knew.

I love you.

ACKNOWLEDGMENT

I acknowledge that everyone has their own opinions, theories, values, and beliefs. I believe in God. I believe He created everything. He loves us and forgives us for our sins. He gave His one and only Son, Jesus Christ, who died for us. He has allowed us to be able to live eternally in Heaven with Him (Genesis 1:1, Romans 5:8, 1 John 1:9, and John 3:16).

I love God and God loves me. He has blessed me gracefully. He has been by my side throughout my life. He has helped me through my crazy times. He has forgiven me for my sins and mistakes. He has helped me overcome depression and anxiety. He is my rock and my

i

strength. He is my protector and my savior. He loves me and takes great care of me.

I will put him first in everything I do. I will pray and seek his words. I know he will guide me through. I will get my life right with him before it is too late, and I will help others do the same.

PRAYER

Dear God,

Please forgive us for our sins. Please clean our hearts, minds, bodies, and souls. Please guide us in the way we should go. Please help us become the person you created us to be. Please help us get our lives right with you before it's too late. And please help us help others do the same.

Please help us be kind and good to others. And please help others be kind and good to us. Please keep us safe and out of harm's way. Please protect us and shield us from evil. Please guard our hearts, minds, bodies, and souls.

Please help us with our pain and struggles. Please help us with our trials and tribulations. Please help us all spiritually, mentally, emotionally, physically, and financially.

Thank You for watching over us and for protecting us. Thank You for giving us another day. Thank You for Your love, mercy, blessings, and grace. Thank You for providing our daily needs. Thank You, God, for everything.

In Jesus' name, I pray, Amen.

TORNADO

My life is like a tornado

Around and around, it takes me

It spins out of control

It never seems to cease

It started off small

But with every problem it grew

It became ginormous

And suddenly I was consumed

I did not know then

Its growth was determined

On how I responded

I could make it bigger

I could make it smaller

It all depended on

My actions and responses

v

CHAPTER 1 GRANNY AND PAPA

My granny was born on June 12th in Louisiana. She had eight sisters and one brother. I don't know much about her mom besides she was Creole and I don't know anything about her father. My granny did not talk about them often.

She grew up in poverty and had limited access to jobs and resources. She was taught it was best to marry an older man who could provide and take care of her. So, she got married at the age of 18 to a much older man.

She realized shortly after getting married that she had made a mistake. She left her hometown, her husband, her family, and friends, and moved to California.

She was a beautiful woman. She had soft dark skin and a huge thick afro. She was a beauty, and she knew it. She held her head high with confidence and she smiled with grace.

My granny was a bad mama jama. "She was as fine as she could be. Her body measurements were perfect in every dimension. She had a figure that sho' nuff got attention. She was poetry in motion. A beautiful sight to see". My granny was a bad mama jama. (Bad Mama Jama, Carl Carlton, 1981).

My granny's oldest sister moved to

California too. She had Thanksgiving dinners at her home in Oakland on 81st Ave. I enjoyed going over to her house and playing with my cousins. We played on the huge play structure in the backyard, ran around the house, and ate delicious food.

My Aunt was a very big woman with a lot of health issues. She was on bed rest and she slept in the living room. We would all grab our plates of food and sit in the living room with her. We prayed and ate dinner together. She passed away when I was a preteen.

My granny's youngest sister also moved to California. She was a real character. She acted like she was a pimp, some type of playa. She was married to a man, but she was attracted to women and women were attracted to her. She dressed like a man, walked like Superfly, and smiled graciously.

I have so many memories of her. She took me, my siblings, and my cousins, to cash in cans for money, she bought now and later candies, and we played pitty-pat and dominoes for them. She cooked meals with me and helped me take care of my mom when she became ill. My aunt passed away after I had given birth to my first child.

I met my granny's brother once when I was a teenager. Me and my oldest cousin stole my granny's neighbor's car. We were walking to the store when we saw the car running with no one inside. My cousin asked me, "Should I take it?" I said yes. We hopped in the car and took off. The car was swerving out of control. We drove on the sidewalk and knocked down some poles. We got on the freeway and headed to the mall to buy a new outfit. We were supposed to be going to her sister's boyfriend's funeral later that day. Her sister was in juvenile hall and we had promised her that we would make an appearance and pay respects for her, but sadly we did not make it to the funeral.

My cousin lost control of the car again. We were swerving all over the freeway. She stopped the car and we hopped out. We started running toward the brick wall on the side of the freeway. My cousin began climbing some bushes to hop over the brick wall. I tried but I kept sinking into the bushes. I was ready to give up but she started yelling, "Come on Nay! You can do it. Keep going, keep going." So, I did and made it over the brick wall. We ran to my granny's youngest sister's house on 82nd Ave in Oakland.

My uncle had just flown into town for a visit and this was our first time meeting him. We told my aunt and uncle what happened and then they started making plans to help us. They were going to fly us out to Las Vegas where my uncle lived to get away because we thought we were going to jail. We didn't go to Vegas. I just wanted to go back home so I did. I did not see my uncle again. He passed away when I became an adult. I did not meet any of my granny's other sisters or her parents.

My papa was born on September 25th in Berkeley, CA. He had two sisters and two brothers. He was a twin and the youngest child.

My papa grew up to be an attractive young man. He was dark-skinned, tall, slender, and had a charming smile. Ladies fell head over heels for him. He was a fly young man who enjoyed having nice things like his older brother.

He got himself in trouble as a teenager and spent some time in juvenile hall for his behavior. He had a daughter, but he was not present in her life. Later on, he entered the Vietnam War and came back home in 1971.

My papa's mother passed away when my mom was pregnant with me. I wish I had a chance to meet her. I heard great things about her from my mom, papa, and aunts. She was mixed with African American and Native American. She was a Christian and had a strong faith in God. She took great care of her home, her husband, and her children.

My papa's father was an African-American man. He was an alcoholic, but a hard worker. He provided for his wife and children, but sadly he died in a car accident when my papa was a child.

My papa's oldest brother was murdered when my papa was a teenager. My uncle enjoyed having nice things like fancy cars and clothes. He obtained those things by selling drugs. He tried to help a friend do the same, but his friend became jealous and killed him. It turned out, he wasn't his friend at all.

My papa's twin brother was a skilled worker. He had multiple jobs on ships and earned enough money to buy nice cars and a house. He got married and had children, but he left his family, home, and cars and no one knows why. He turned to drugs and lived on the streets for the rest of his life.

One day he went into a store on High ST. to buy something. He was short of a nickel, so he headed to the front door to go look for one, when he turned around the store employee shot him in the head. My uncle became a vegetable. He had to learn to walk and talk all over again.

My uncle passed away when I was a teenager. I remembered the day my mom received the news. She sat on our living room couch crying. I recall this being in December close to Christmas because we were decorating our home and Christmas tree. She played Mariah Carey Fly Like a Bird over and over again in remembrance of him.

My papa's oldest sister was known as the one who did not play. You did not want to get on her bad side or into trouble. She was blunt and honest. She told things how they were and never sugarcoated anything. My mom resembled her in so many ways. I believe that is why she was my mom's favorite Aunt.

I enjoyed going to her house for Thanksgiving and Christmas dinners. She cooked huge and delicious dinners for everyone to enjoy. I used to go to my Aunt's house to help her clean out her cupboards. I enjoyed doing something kind for her and seeing a huge smile on her face.

My papa's youngest sister was a sweet and kind lady. She bought me and my sister a women's bible and encouraged us to believe and trust in the Lord. I remember when I was a teenager, I asked to visit her in Missouri and she said yes. My papa paid for my plane ticket.

I enjoyed myself so much that I wanted to stay. She asked me why and I told her about all my problems back home. She said, "You can't run away from your problems. They will follow you wherever you go. You have to face them and find a solution. God can help you if you ask him."

I was so upset and sad when she said this. I thought staying with her would be the best thing for me at that time. But now I understand what she meant. I realize I was my biggest problem and unless I changed my mindset and my ways, my problems will always be with me.

My papa and granny met shortly after my papa returned from the war. They started a relationship with all their childhood trauma and their flaws. My papa was an absent father to his daughter from a previous relationship and my granny was a married woman. They both were alcoholics and drug addicts.

My papa started off drinking alcohol, and then he tried weed, heroin, and speed. My papa once said, "A good drug dealer knows how to get you hooked. He starts off by giving you a free sample, a small taste. And once you felt that good high, you would come back begging for more." His drug dealer was a good one and he had my papa hooked. My granny started drinking and using drugs once she got to California.

My papa and granny loved each other passionately. They expressed their love for one another the only way they knew how. My papa was very attentive and caring toward my granny when she was pregnant. He ran her bath water, rubbed an oatmeal treatment all over her skin, and massaged her feet gently. He cared for and loved her so much that he would wake up in the middle of the night and rush to the store to get whatever she was craving at that moment.

My grandparents had two daughters together, my mom and Anne. My mom was born on June 9th and my Anne was born on November 13th. People thought they were twins, but they were born two years apart.

My granny splurged on my mom and Anne. Instead of paying bills, she used her money to take them on shopping sprees. She wanted her children to have the things she did not have when she was younger. This behavior led them to be homeless and sleeping in cars. My papa spent whatever money he had on drugs and his behavior was another reason why they were homeless and sleeping in cars.

Domestic violence was another dynamic in their relationship and my granny was the abuser. One night, she convinced her younger sister to set my papa on fire while he slept in bed. He woke up surrounded by flames. He called her a crazy woman, but he did not leave. He stayed.

I was shocked when I heard this story. I wondered why would she do that to a person she loved and why did he stay. Then I thought a crazy woman must be something nice.

A crazy woman was what she was called. A crazy woman was what followed us all. A crazy woman spiced things up and loved passionately. This depiction of a woman was glorified in our family, and this was the type of woman I wanted to be.

My papa was sent to Santa Rita jail when my mom and Anne were teenagers. He learned about God while he was there. He got baptized, came home, and was set on turning his life around, but my granny was not. She wanted to continue drinking, gambling, and doing drugs.

One day my granny had given my mom and Anne permission to have a house party. My papa was not fond of it and said, "If they have this party, I am leaving and never coming back." My mom and Anne ended up having the party, and my papa left and did not return.

My papa was the first person I recall breaking a generational curse in our family. He stopped drinking and using drugs. He turned his life over to God and never turned back. He continued to take care of my mom and Anne, but he did not let anyone turn him back to his old ways.

Thank you, God, for allowing my papa to draw close to you, to learn of you, and to know you. Thank you for turning his life around. Thank you for changing his ways. Thank you for saving him and for showing him grace.

He is a better man because of you. Thank you for allowing me to share his testimony. Please continue to help us all on our spiritual journey. In Jesus' name, I pray, Amen.

CHAPTER 2 MOM AND DAD

My mom was born and raised in East Oakland, CA. My dad was born in Wichita, Kansas, but he moved to East Oakland when he was 5 years old. East Oakland is our home. It is the place where my parents met and the place where I grew up.

My mom was eighteen and my dad was twenty when they first met. My dad showed interest in my mom, but she did not reciprocate the same interest. She had just broken up with her boyfriend and my dad was not her type. They both were Geminis and it seemed unlikely that they would get along. Even though my mom was not interested in my dad, he continued to pursue her until she finally gave him a chance.

My mom took a pregnancy test a few months later, and it was positive. She was pregnant with me, and she was afraid of becoming a teenage mom, afraid of telling her parents, and afraid of telling my dad.

I was her first child and my dad's second child. He already had a daughter with another woman before meeting my mom and he was not a present parent in her life. My sister was raised by our dad's mother. Our grandmother took care of my sister because our dad was an absentee parent and my sister's mother was on drugs and a prostitute.

My mom went to Anne and told her the

news. She said, "I'm pregnant, and I don't know what to do. I'm scared to tell him." Anne said, "Call him and I will be right here if he acts a fool."

My mom picked up the phone and dialed my dad's number. He answered and said, "Hello?" She took a deep breath and said, "I'm pregnant." They were silent for a few seconds and then he asked, "Are you sure?" She replied, "Yes, I'm sure. I took a pregnancy test and it's positive." He said, "Okay, what do you want to do?" She replied, "I don't know. I'm scared." He said, "Well, I'm okay with whatever decision you make, but I do want us to keep the baby."

My mom thought about how she wasn't

ready to have a baby, but she also did not want to have an abortion. My mom said, "Okay, I'm going to keep the baby." My dad started yelling "I'm going to be a dad again! I'm going to be a dad again!" Anne asked, "What is he saying? Do I need to curse him out?" My mom replied, "No, he's happy." Anne was shocked and my mom was too.

My mom thought my dad would act like Anne's babies' daddies. She thought he would deny her child and break up with her. Anne gave birth to her first child when she was sixteen and the father was an absent parent. She had gotten pregnant again at seventeen by a different boy and he was also an absent parent. My mom thought about how my dad was an absent parent to his first child and she was worried he would be an absent parent in my life too.

My dad got back on the phone and said, "I'm so happy we are having a baby together." He asked, "How are you doing? Do you need anything?" My mom replied, "I'm okay. I don't need anything." He said, "Okay, I'll come over later. I love you." She replied, "I love you too" and hung up the phone.

My mom felt relieved knowing my dad was happy she was pregnant, but then she remembered she had to tell her parents. My granny was thrilled about the news, but my papa was not. He did not like his daughters having children at a young age even though my mom was eighteen. He was a man of God now and he wanted to teach his children God's ways. He wanted them to get married before they engaged in sexual activity and had babies.

My dad was very caring and attentive toward my mom during her pregnancy. He was very loving, patient, and kind. He did the same things my papa did for my granny when she was pregnant. He ran her bath water, rubbed an oatmeal treatment all over her skin, and massaged her feet gently. He cared for and loved her so much that he would even wake up in the middle of the night and rush to the store to get whatever she was craving at that moment.

I was born on October 12th. I was a very

chunky baby. I weighed 10 lbs. My mom and dad said I was so quiet, they forgot I was around sometimes.

We lived with my granny for a few months on Fruitvale Ave in East Oakland, CA. My mom and dad did not have a job. They submitted job applications, but they were not successful in obtaining employment. My mom applied for welfare, and she received about $300 a month from cash aid and $200 a month in food stamps.

My mom was not getting enough from welfare to take care of themselves and me. So, my dad started selling drugs. It was illegal and very risky, but it was a risk he was willing to take. It was a way for him to be able to take care of himself and his family.

My parents paid my granny's rent, bills, and bought groceries. My granny wanted more money, but my parents told her no. She became infuriated and decided to put us out. My granny tossed all our stuff out into the street. My mom and dad collected our things, called a cab, and went to a motel on MacArthur Blvd. My mom was able to use her resources from the welfare office to obtain an apartment.

CHAPTER 3 72ND HAMILTON

My mom and dad got their first apartment together on 72nd and Hamilton, in East Oakland, CA. It was a one-bedroom apartment filled with roaches. They felt blessed and grateful to have a place to live, but they wished they lived somewhere better.

One night my dad came home bloody and beat up. He was unrecognizable. He looked like a monster. I started to cry because I was scared, and he was in so much pain.

One of Anne's baby daddies and his friends jumped my dad. Her baby daddy did not like that my dad moved into their neighborhood and started selling drugs. He did not want the competition and decided to send my dad a message.

My mom gave my dad ice and pain medication. He laid in her arms while she comforted him. My dad continued to sell drugs to provide and take care of his family.

Another night, my dad found out his best friend was murdered. We all sat on the floor together while my dad cried. I wiped away his tears while my mom held him in her arms. This was another night I watched my mom comfort him.

My mom and dad were known as a ride-or-die couple. They were compared to Bonnie and Clyde. They bought guns to protect themselves and their family. My mom and dad wore black trench coats with their guns underneath when they went outside. My mom jumped into my dad's fights whenever he got into one and she was nearby.

They loved each other passionately and protected each other fiercely. People wanted a relationship like theirs. They were looking at their relationship from the outside. Not fully aware of what was going on inside.

My mom became pregnant with my younger sister and she gave birth to her on October 6th. I was a few days short of turning a year old. My sister was a beautiful baby. She had a head full of hair and caramelized skin. She received a lot of compliments from family, friends, and strangers.

My mom was not attentive or nurturing toward my sister. My dad mostly took care of her. He changed her and fed her. My sister would stay in her crib all day without being fed or changed until my dad came home.

My parents started to argue more often, and my dad started putting his hands on my mom. He used to beat her to the point where she had to go to the hospital for black eyes, a busted nose, or broken bones. My mom did not leave him though. She stayed.

I used to tell myself I would never be with a man like that. I would never let a man hurt me or put his hands on me. It's crazy how when we're younger, we swear about all the things we would not do, and we end up doing them anyway.

My mom became pregnant with my brother and he was born on September 18th. He was also a cute baby. He had caramelized skin and a head full of hair. People complimented him a lot too. They said he was very handsome and cute.

I dropped my baby brother by accident the first time I held him. He was so small. He slipped right through my arms and fell onto the floor. He cried, but my parents did not take him to see a doctor. My mom picked him up and whispered, "Shhh" while swaying him back and forth. I remember seeing the difference in how my mom treated all of us. She was a mother to me and my brother, but she was not a mother to my younger sister.

I wanted to believe my brother was okay, but I did not know for sure. To this day, I wonder if I damaged him and his brain. I wonder if I caused any distress that he took into adulthood. I wonder if his struggles in life were caused by me.

I did not like living in our one-bedroom apartment filled with roaches. Me and my brother slept in the same bed with my mom and dad while my sister slept in the baby crib.

One night I woke up and saw our walls covered with roaches. My dad's leg was hanging off the bed and it was so close to touching the wall. I started to cry and scream while trying to pull Dad's leg back onto the bed. I did not want the roaches to get us.

Another day, I grabbed a box of raisin bran cereal and sat on the front porch. I pulled the bag out of the box and saw the raisins moving. As I continued to observe the movement, I realized it wasn't raisins, it was roaches. I never wanted or ate raisin bran again.

Our apartment was raided so many times. The police would kick in our door and run into our apartment with their guns out. When I was younger, I did not understand why the police were there so often and why they entered our apartment the way they did.

One day, the police raided our apartment while my dad's friend Sam was at our home fixing the heater. The police busted down our door and Sam ran and tried to hide under the bed. I thought it was weird that he was trying to hide.

The police ransacked our apartment. They searched the kitchen and the bathroom. They flipped the beds and the couches. They even checked the wall heater Sam was trying to fix.

My mom and dad were arrested on drug charges and Sam was released. My granny moved from Fruitvale Ave to a house across the street from us. So, my siblings and I stayed with her until my mom and dad were released. My parents came home a few months later and we went right back to living the same lifestyle.

I grew up hating guns because I had a traumatic experience with my mom shooting my oldest cousin in the stomach. We went across the street to my granny's house for a visit. I sat in front of the television with my siblings and cousins watching cartoons.

As we gazed at the T.V., my cousin who's two years older than me said "Ouch" very softly. And then he began to say, "Ouch" more loudly. We all looked at him to see what was wrong and saw him holding his stomach and blood around his hands.

My mom was sitting in a chair cleaning her gun when it went off. It still had bullets in the chamber. Someone called 911 to get my cousin to the hospital. I'm not sure what they told the police and doctors about how he got shot, but my mom did not go to jail or prison for it.

CHAPTER 4 77TH GREENSIDE

My mom received her first Section 8 voucher when I was 5 years old. We moved to a 3-bedroom apartment on 77th and Bancroft. The apartments were green, and the area was known as Greenside. We had more space, but the apartment had roaches and rats, and it was located in a high-crime neighborhood.

I still liked our new place though. My mom and dad had their room, my sister and I shared a room, and my brother had a room to himself. We were only allowed to play on our patio. We were not allowed to go beyond the patio because of the high crime, violence, and drugs. So, we mostly stayed in the apartment using our imagination and finding creative things to do.

My favorite game to play was school. I always wanted to be the teacher, and my siblings and cousins to be the students. I taught them things I learned from T.V. I taught them math and how to read.

Sometimes they did not want to play, and I cried to my dad about it. He would say, "Sorry baby girl. You cannot make them play. You cannot make them do things they don't want to do. It's great that you want to teach them and help them learn. Maybe they will want to play some other day" And then I would say, "Okay, Daddy, but I can't wait to go to school." And luckily for me, starting elementary was approaching.

My mom took me to school on my first day of kindergarten. We drove to Webster Academy and as soon as she parked, I said, "Bye Mom" and tried to hop out of the car. She said, "Wait, I have to take you to your class."

I thought I could find my way around the school like the kids did on the T.V. shows and movies I watched at home. We got out of the car and walked through the school gate. We went to the office to find out where my class was located and who my teacher was.

We walked to my classroom and there was a white lady with curly hair standing by the door. She said, "Hi, how are you?" My mom replied, "Hi, we're fine. How are you?" The teacher said, "I'm well. Thanks for asking."

Then she looked down at me and asked, "What is your name?" I said, "Tajanee Ford."

The teacher asked me a series of questions. She asked, "Can you say the alphabet, how many numbers can you count up to, can you read, and can you spell your name?" She was impressed by how much I knew. She told my mom she did not think I should be in kindergarten. She recommended that I be moved up to first grade. My mom did not agree. So, I stayed.

My kindergarten teacher was very nice and I enjoyed spending time with her. I had gotten so attached to her. I was sad when she had to go on maternity leave.

Back at home, my family started calling my brother weird and gay. One day my dad said he wanted to spend some quality time with his Junior. So, he took my brother with him to hang out with his friends.

My dad came back home and told my mom he was not taking my brother anywhere else ever again. He said, "He was acting weird. The whole time he was staring under cars." My mom said, "He's a little boy. He's curious about the world. He was probably curious about cars." My dad said," I could understand if he looked under there for a few minutes but he bent over and stared under the cars for hours. He looked weird and everybody laughed at us."

My brother spent a lot of time playing

with me and my sister. We played with dolls and dressed up. My dad was furious when he saw my brother wearing our dresses, heels, and my mom's makeup. He said, "Stop acting like a faggot and shit. Are you gay? Do you want to be gay? Take that shit off and I better not ever see you in it again".

I didn't know what faggot or gay meant. I thought my brother was just trying to have fun and play the games me and my sister wanted to play. He was having fun until my dad came in. His face dropped and he slowly took off the clothes and heels and walked back into his room.

My mom continued to abuse my sister. She cooked food for everyone in the house except for my sister. I used to sneak into the kitchen, grab some food and hide food under my clothes, walk back to my room, and feed my sister. One day I caught my sister drinking out of the toilet. I walked up to her and asked why was she doing that. She said she was thirsty.

My mom used to tell my sister, "I don't love you. I don't even like you. I hate you. You are so ugly. Nobody is going to want you. Nobody likes you." As we got older, she started to say, "You better learn how to have great sex and suck dick really good because that is the only way you will be able to get and keep a man."

My mom combed all of our hair and she

bought all of us nice clothes and shoes. On the outside, we looked like we were well taken care of. We were always clean and had new Jordans. But on the inside, we were hurting emotionally and mentally.

I hated the way my mom treated my sister. I didn't understand how she could treat her child, her flesh and blood so badly. I always questioned what was wrong with her. Why was she so mean? Why did she hate my sister so much? I wanted to protect my sister and help her. I wanted to take care of her, but sometimes I felt helpless. There wasn't much for me to do at a young age.

Our first Christmas in our new apartment was the best. My mom and dad bought a Christmas tree and some decorations. We all decorated the apartment and the Christmas tree.

We placed clear, red, and green bowls on the living room table and filled them with candy. We hung stockings on the walls and decorated the tree with clear, red, and green ornaments, and we placed different colored candy canes around the tree.

My dad picked me up to put the Christmas star on top of the tree. The Christmas star was also clear, red, and green and it blinked on and off. It was a beautiful Christmas tree topper.

We played Christmas songs, laughed,

and danced around the apartment. We all

seemed so happy. My parents were not

arguing, fighting, or drinking. They were

smiling and laughing. This was the best

Christmas we had so far. This was my favorite

Christmas of all.

CHAPTER 5 PRISON

The Christmas joy quickly faded away as my mom and dad started arguing again. My mom became pregnant with my youngest brother. One day, my mom and dad were in their bedroom arguing. My dad pulled out a belt and started to whoop my mom with it while she tried to retreat to their bedroom closet. He walked out of their room and then out of the apartment.

I walked into my parent's room and heard my mom crying in the closet. I slowly started to walk toward the closet door, and she began to yell, "Get out! Get out! Get out!" I jumped back and ran out of the room. I wanted to hold her, comfort her, and wipe her tears, but she needed and wanted her space, so I let her be. She went to the hospital later that night and gave birth to my baby brother.

My youngest brother was born on October 25th. He was a petite baby. Everyone said he looked like an old man.

My parents got back together, and they continued to drink, argue, and fight. My mom started seeing another man and my dad found out about it. They had an intense argument and then my dad left to confront the man my mom was cheating with.

The man and his family jumped my dad. My dad came back home bloody with knots all over his head. He grabbed his guns and went back out the door.

He later returned and yelled at me "Go get your backpack!" So, I ran into my room, grabbed my purple princess backpack, and ran back to my dad. I watched him as he loaded his guns into my backpack.

My mom packed some things and we all got into the car and drove off toward Eastmont Mall. My dad made a left turn on Church Street and parked. Police surrounded us, and they were yelling, "Put your hands up and get out of the car!" My mom yelled back, "We have kids in the car!"

My mom and dad put their hands up and slowly got out of the car. They both laid on the ground while the police slowly walked toward them with their guns drawn. The police placed handcuffs on their arms, picked them up, and placed them in the back of separate police cars.

My siblings and I sat on the sidewalk as we waited for my granny and Anne to pick us up. My mom went to jail for a few months for a warrant, and my dad was sentenced to 6 years in prison for attempted murder. He shot one of the man's family members' arms off.

CHAPTER 6 LIVING WITHOUT DAD

My three siblings and I lived with my granny, Anne, and her four kids while we waited for my mom to be released from jail. My granny moved from 72nd and Hamilton to 79th and Bancroft which was two blocks from my mom's apartment.

I did not like living at my granny's house. My granny and Anne told stories about alligators and snakes living in their basement. I was afraid to be there.

One day, I thought my sister was going to die. Everyone was sitting in the living room eating dinner and watching T.V. My sister was eating a lot and her stomach started to expand. My granny and Anne made comments that her stomach was about to burst.

My sister was only a year younger than me, but she was so small and short. She looked malnourished. At my granny's house, she finally was able to eat and she ate a lot. I touched her belly and it was so hard.

I started to cry. I said, "Please slow down. Please stop eating. You had enough. Your stomach is about to pop. You can have more later. Please stop" She looked at me and stopped eating.

I was 6 years old when I started taking care of myself and my siblings. I cleaned, cooked, changed diapers, made bottles, and fed my baby brother. I took on these responsibilities because my granny and Anne were not doing it and it needed to be done. Someone had to do it. So, I did.

One day, my sister, brother, and I were playing outside with a few of our cousins. We noticed flames coming from one of the bedroom windows. One of my cousins was in the house playing with matches under the bed. The bed caught fire, and she got scared and ran into another room.

Anne ran outside the house holding my baby brother by the arm in one hand and her youngest daughter in the other hand. She sat them on the sidewalk and ran back into the house to look for my cousin. She found her hiding in one of the rooms, grabbed her, and ran back outside.

We all sat on the sidewalk as we waited for the fire department to come. We watched my granny's house burn to the ground. We gathered what we could and walked two blocks down the street to my mom's apartment.

Anne unlocked the door and we all walked in. The apartment stunk badly and it was a mess. There was raw fish in the sink which was supposed to be our dinner the day my parents were arrested.

The police searched our apartment and they flipped over the couches and mattresses, emptied our fridge and cabinets, and threw our clothes on the floor. My granny and Anne did not clean up the mess.

A few days later a white lady came to our apartment. She took a look around and talked to my granny and Anne for a few minutes. Then she took each kid one by one into one of the bedrooms to interview.

It was my turn and she asked me a few questions. She asked, "How do you like living here? Are your grandmother and Aunt nice to you? Do they take good care of you? Do they hurt you? How do they discipline you? I answered all her questions and when I was done, she continued interviewing the other children.

She completed her interviews and talked to my granny and Anne once more. She told them to clean up the house and buy some groceries. She said she would be back to visit again and then she left.

Anne asked each of us what did the lady say. I told her the questions the lady asked and my responses. I said, "I told her I do like living here even though we have roaches and rats. You guys take good care of us and only whoop us if we get in trouble."

Anne yelled at me. She said, "Why would you say that?! Why would you tell her our business?" I said, "I don't know. I thought I was supposed to tell the truth." Anne said, "Didn't your mama and daddy tell you to not tell people y'all business, especially white folks? She might come back here and take y'all away. Well, that's not my fault if she does."

My cousins started laughing at me and called me stupid. I felt stupid and ashamed. I started to question myself. I thought, how could I be so dumb? How could I put me and my siblings in a messed-up situation? Why wasn't I smart? Why wasn't I more like Anne's kids?

After this, I no longer wanted to talk again. I was already shy, quiet, and reserved and this made me want to stay that way forever. I stopped engaging in conversations because I did not want to say the wrong thing or sound stupid.

I believe I did the right thing by telling the truth. Sometimes there are consequences when you tell the truth, but I believe the consequences may be worse if you lie.

A few days later there was a knock on the door. I asked, "Who is it?" and it was my mom. I opened the door and jumped on her. I gave her a tight hug and she squeezed me back. We walked into the apartment together.

She looked around and said, "What the hell? Why does it look and smell like this?" Anne and Granny said, "The police did it." My mom responded, "And y'all didn't bother to clean up? It has been months since the police have been here. Have y'all been living and sleeping in filth? This is crazy. Get up and clean my house now!"

I was so happy to hear that. I did not like living in a dirty place. I tried my best to clean up as much as I could while she was gone, but it was too much to clean for one person. She came home and made everyone clean up. I was so thrilled to have her back. My mom was not the best, but she kept a clean apartment, and I was happy about that.

Saturday mornings my siblings and I woke up early, made a bowl of cereal, and watched cartoons until my mom woke up. She would wake up, turn on the stereo, put on some music, and clean the apartment. I started to help her clean too. We washed the laundry, cleaned the kitchen, dining room, and living room, and cleaned the bedrooms and bathrooms. I enjoyed those moments with her.

Sunday mornings my siblings, cousins, and I went to church with our papa. We attended Sunday school and church service. We were at the church building from 9 a.m. to 12:30 p.m., sometimes until 1:00 p.m.

I enjoyed learning about God, singing hymns, and being surrounded by Christians. I also enjoyed spending time with my papa, siblings, and cousins in a spiritual setting. Going to church always made me feel calm and peaceful.

My uncle, my dad's best friend, helped my mom while my dad was in prison. He gave her rides to the grocery stores, to pay bills, and buy a Christmas tree, and presents.

He also gave me money for my report cards. I already enjoyed school, but I loved it even more when I started getting paid for my good grades. He wanted to make sure we were okay while my dad was away.

Me and my sister enjoyed spending time with our aunt, my mom's older half-sister. She would come pick us up and let us spend the weekend at her apartment. We ate tasty food and played games with our cousins.

I adored and admired my auntie. She was beautiful with straight black hair. She had class and she was intelligent. She was married and had three boys at that time. I wanted to be like her. I wanted to have a life like hers. She seemed so happy and in love. I wanted a beautiful home, with a loving husband, and loving children.

My mom's best friend was my godmother. She reminded me of the singer Brandy from Moesha. To me, they looked just alike. She was happy to be my god mom and I was happy to have her in my life.

I missed my dad. Even though he was an alcoholic and an abuser, I was still a daddy's girl. He called me his twin because I looked just like him. He gave me a nickname, Blackabelly, because of my dark skin.

He continued to provide for me and my siblings while he was in prison. He wrote us letters and bought us Christmas and birthday gifts. My siblings and I visited him a few times with my grandmother. My mom was not allowed to visit because she was on probation.

One day one of my mom's friends and her children came over to our apartment for a visit. One of her sons said some disrespectful things about my dad. I became so angry. I went into the kitchen, grabbed a skillet, and hit him upside the head with it. I did not play about my dad.

Dear Daddy

Heart full of dreams
of things I want and need
but mostly you
can make my heart from being blue
I need you to be by my side
so, you can exemplify
me as an intelligent person
Thank you, Daddy,
for helping me believe in myself
to be a sentry
to my life, mind, body, and heart
I say mean things to you
but none of them are true
You are my solider and my father
With you and God by my side, I'll never suffer
I want you to know
You are my twin
With us together the devil will never win
My mind is staid
on making you proud
But let's be patient
because it will take a while
All our dreams will come true
I will be on TV giving thanks to you
for when I messed up, you still cared
You still showed me, love,
and when I didn't listen
to your words, you still shared
Thank you for not giving up on me
So, I will always love you, Daddy

CHAPTER 7 DYSFUNCTIONAL

My family praised me for my respectfulness and intelligence. They told me I was very smart and had a lot of potential to do great things. They said, "Keep doing good in school. You are going to be someone great someday." But I slowly stopped wanting to be the smart one with a lot of potential. I wanted to be like the rest of our family who got praised every day for the things they did.

My family frequently praised those who committed crimes, sold drugs, did robberies, and were in fights. My oldest cousin followed in his dad's footsteps. He started selling drugs, robbing homes, and stealing at six years old. He would come home with a lot of money and jewelry. My granny, mom, and Anne were so happy and praised him. He continued to do it because he saw it was a good thing to do to provide for his family. He was in and out of juvenile hall for his crimes and that became his norm.

My cousin took my youngest brother with him a lot. They would stay out all day together while my cousin sold drugs, robbed homes, smoked weed, and played dice. He introduced my brother to that lifestyle.

My brother was a baby when our dad went to prison, so he didn't know him. My cousin became his role model. My mom, granny, and Anne used to tell my brother that he was the man of the house now that my dad was gone. Can you imagine the pressure he must have felt? He was a little boy. He should have been able to enjoy his childhood instead of trying to take care of a family.

My oldest cousin's sister was praised for fighting. She liked to argue and fight. My family always asked her, "Did you win? Did you take off first?" She always had to hit the other person first and she always had to win the fights. She was known as the fighter in the family.

My mom continued to drink and pass out. One day my youngest brother was in the room with her while she was passed out drunk, and he started a fire in her bed. My mom woke up covered in flames. She jumped out of bed, filled a pot with water, ran back into her room, and threw the water on her bed. She continued to drink and pass out.

My granny and Annie moved out of our apartment and moved into another apartment on 71st and Hamilton. My siblings and I still were not allowed to go outside to play. We were only allowed to play on the patio. We would stand on the patio fence and watch the neighborhood kids play outside.

One day, we were playing on the patio and standing up on the fence when my mom called us to come into the apartment. As we were getting down, bullets started to fly over our heads and into the apartment.

Another day we heard gunshots and dropped to the floor. Shortly after, we heard people talking outside our front door. We opened it and saw a man bleeding from gunshot wounds. We saw him take his last breath.

There was a lady who had four children who lived in the apartment complex. She had two girls and two boys. Her daughters were older than her boys just like my mom's children. They invited me over to their apartment one day to hang out and spend the night.

Me and the oldest daughter slept on the couch in the living room. I woke up in the middle of the night and saw her daughter watching porn. She was hovering over me with her hands in her pants. I never went over there again.

One of the lady's boys was a menace in the neighborhood. He used to cause so much chaos. One day he came to our front door and was trying to fight my youngest brother. The boy was about five or six years old trying to fight my three-year-old brother. I went into my mom's room, grabbed a belt, and held it behind my back. I swung the belt across his face when he got close to our door. He ran home crying.

A few minutes later his mom came to our door. She said she was going to beat my ass. So, I went into the kitchen, grabbed a knife, and went back to the front door. I held the knife out toward her and told her I was going to cut her if she tried to touch me. I told her to keep her badass kids away from me and my family.

One day, my mom wanted me to walk to a store a few blocks from the apartment. I hated going outside. I did not want to run into the neighborhood menaces. I walked to the store and picked up a glass bottle on my way back home. I picked it up for protection. As I got closer to the apartments, the lady's son saw me and started running toward me. I hid the bottle behind my back and when he came close enough, I threw it at him and ran home.

I no longer liked living there. I didn't

feel safe. Other things were going on in the neighborhood besides having issues with the lady and her kids.

In this neighborhood, a boy was killed over a dollar while playing dice. A girl put a firecracker in a little man's pants, someone threw a snake through our kitchen window, and Anne was jumped by some girls who lived in the apartments. Everything in this neighborhood instilled fear in me. I feared going outside. I feared going on the patio. I feared living in those apartments.

Anne got an apartment on 106th and Apricot. She lived in an apartment underneath my papa's apartment. I enjoyed going over to her place. We played Crash and Sonic on

Nintendo. We also read bible scriptures and sang hymn songs together. Me and my cousins walked to the penny store to buy candy and we walked to McDonalds for breakfast.

Anne threw my oldest cousin a birthday party at her new place. We jumped in the jumper, played jump rope, danced, and had cake. An ice cream truck came down the street and we crossed the street to buy some ice cream.

A car came down the street when I was crossing to go back to Anne's apartment. The person driving the car stopped to let me cross and then hit me when I was in the middle of their front bumper. I got up and they hit me again. I got up a second time and limped across the street.

My oldest cousin started yelling, "Did he hit you, Nay?! Did he hit you?!" I tried to mutter yes as I slowly limped inside. My cousin began hitting the car and yelling at the driver to get out. The driver drove off quickly. My mom did not take me to the hospital or call the police. Everyone went back to enjoying the party like nothing happened.

CHAPTER 8 MOM'S BOYFRIENDS

My mom started dating other men while my dad was in prison. She dated a Jamaican man for a few months. Everyone thought he was attractive. She began to think he was seeing other women. She got upset, started an argument, and busted the windows out of his car. We did not see him again after that.

One day my mom brought home a Mexican man. He was short and didn't speak English well. He bought my mom and himself some alcohol and he bought me and my siblings some food and drinks. They got drunk, laughed, and danced.

His wife called his phone and he

answered. He kept saying, "Shh," to us while he tried to talk to her. She must have heard us in the background because she asked to speak to my mom. She told my mom they were married and had children together. She became angry and called my mom a bitch. Her husband hung up the phone and left our apartment. We never saw him again.

My mom started dating another Mexican man. He was short and stocky. He loved the Oakland Raiders. He always wore a Raiders hat and jersey.

One night her boyfriend was going to the store, and I asked if I could go with him. He said yes and told me to hurry up. I ran into my room, grabbed my jacket and shoes, and ran back into the living room huffing and puffing. He was standing by the door waiting for me.

We walked out the door and to his car. I jumped in the front seat, and we drove to the store. I was excited. I was thinking about all the snacks and treats I wanted to get for me and my siblings.

We parked by the store and walked inside. I grabbed some chips, cupcakes, and juice. He paid for everything, and we walked back to the car.

As I was trying to grab my seat belt to buckle up, he placed his hand on my left leg. I slowly turned around and stared out at the windshield. He moved his hand up my leg and between my legs. He reached over my seat, placed his left hand on my right cheek, and pulled it toward him. He brought his face toward mine and started to kiss my lips. I closed my eyes and tried to contemplate what was going on and why it was happening. I was not sure what to do so I stayed quiet and still.

He moved his hand away from my face and moved back from my lips. I quickly turned my head toward the windshield and buckled my seatbelt. We drove back home in silence.

I quickly got out of the car and ran into my room. I sat on my bed still thinking about what just happened. My younger sister was in the room, and she asked, "What's wrong with

you?" I told her what happened, and she said,
"You have to tell Mama."

So, I wrote down what had happened
on a piece of paper. I walked into the living
room and handed the letter to my mom and
walked back into my room. A few minutes later
my mom called me. I walked out of my room
and into the dining room. She was sitting on
his lap. She held up my letter and asked, "Is
this true?" I replied, "Yes." She said, "No, it's
not. You are a liar. You just want me to get
back with your daddy."

I felt a sharp pain in my chest. Tears
started to rise in my ears and roll down my
cheeks. I was so hurt and shocked by her
response. I yelled, "It is true!" And she yelled

back, "No it's not. Stop lying Nay." We continued yelling back and forth to each other until I ran outside of the apartment. I ran from 77th and Bancroft to my granny's apartment on 71st and Hamilton.

Anne let me in, and I told her what happened. She immediately called my mom and cursed her out. She said, "What kind of mother are you? How can you believe a man over your child?"

I confided in Anne from that point on. I talked to her about everything. I talked to her about my interests in movies, shows, romance, and boys. I talked to her about my dreams and goals. I talked about things I was struggling with or excited about.

I confided in her with everything until she used my words to hurt me. She started to talk badly about me to other people. And when she got mad at me, she would say, "That's why your mama doesn't love you. That's why she believed a man over you. No one likes you or loves you." She said horrible things to her children and my siblings too.

So, I went back to being quiet and reserved. I had trust and communication issues. I felt like there was no point in talking to people. They will either not believe me, or they will use what I tell them to hurt me.

CHAPTER 9 ATTENTION

My papa picked me and my sister up to help him clean his kitchen. We went to his house and cleaned his refrigerator and stove. He gave us a few dollars to help him clean.

He took us to Blockbuster to rent some movies and to Papa Murphy's to grab some pizza. We drove back to his home, placed the pizza in the oven, and put the VHS into the VCR. We were appreciative to earn some money and be able to spend time with him.

My papa had been taking me, my siblings, and my cousins to church since we were babies. My older cousin decided she was ready to get baptized and I wanted to follow her and get baptized too.

We did a few bible studies with our preacher and then the day came to be baptized. We both were baptized on the same day. I was eight years old, and she was nine. A sister in the church took us to Macy's and bought us a dress. I picked out a purple dress with flowers. I loved that dress and purple became my favorite color. She also bought us a diary.

I used my diary to get my mom's attention. I would grab my diary and a pencil, run into my mom's room, and sit near her bed. I would write, smile, and laugh. I would make so much noise to get her attention, but she never showed any curiosity. She never asked,

"What are you writing about or what is so funny?"

I started writing about kissing boys and having a boyfriend. One day my cousins came to my school to get me, and they said, "You're in so much trouble." I kept asking, "Why?" but they would not tell me.

When I got home my mom said, "Let's go to my room." We walked into her room, and she shut the door. She said, "Is this true?" while holding up my diary. I asked, "Is what true?" She said, "Don't play with me, Nay. The things you wrote here. Are they true?" I responded, "Yes, some of it." She said, "What about the boys? Is the stuff about the boys true?" I said, "No." She said, "If it's not true, then why did you write it?" I said, "Because I wanted to get your attention." She said, "I don't believe you. Go in your room and wait for me."

I opened her door and walked down the hall into my room. I could hear my siblings and cousins whispering and laughing. After a few minutes, my mom came into my room with her belt. I started screaming and crying. I said, "I am telling the truth! I am telling the truth." But she didn't listen. She whooped me anyway.

And then I realized I was a liar. I lied in my diary. I should not have written those things. That was not the attention I wanted. I wrote lies and she believed those lies. So, I deserved what I got.

I was bullied at home and in school. I was bullied by my older cousin. She would hit me and call me ugly. She said she was pretty because she had lighter skin and I was ugly because I had dark skin.

At school, kids called me a tar baby. They said I was ugly because my skin was so dark, I had a big nose, big lips, big hands, big feet, and a big forehead.

I was so insecure about the way I looked. I wanted lighter skin, a smaller nose, and smaller lips. And a smaller forehead. I wished I could change the way I looked. I remember watching the movie Selena and wishing I was Mexican.

I felt like no one loved me or even liked me. I wanted someone to love me unconditionally. I watched romantic shows and movies and became infatuated with love. But the T.V. shows and movies were fantasies. That love wasn't real, but I still yearned for it.

In fourth grade, I ran for vice president, and I won. I was so proud of myself. I also became a hall monitor and a tutor. I went to my younger brother's class a few times a week to read to him and his classmates.

I joined the school Christmas play and attended all the rehearsals. I was so excited about the show, but when the big night came, my mom was too drunk to go. She drank so much that she passed out, so I stayed home.

I started having trouble with my hearing. I was so embarrassed about it that I stopped attending the student council meetings, and I stopped being the hall monitor and tutor. I lost interest in a lot of things.

CHAPTER 10 48TH YGNACIO

A new home could mean a lot of things. New space, new ambiance, new opportunities, friends, school, and environment. I was so excited to move to 47th and Ygnacio. I was ten years old when we moved into our new apartment.

My mom always made big Thanksgiving and Christmas dinners but now that I was ten, she allowed me to help her with them. She taught me how to cook and she learned how to cook from my papa. I enjoyed learning from her, cooking with her, and spending time with her. We used to cook; ham, turkey, some greens with ham hocks or neckbones, black eye peas with ham hocks or neckbones and okra, baked macaroni and cheese, candied yams, cornbread, 2 sweet potato pie, 1 German chocolate cake and one yellow cake with chocolate frosting. We also made a Jello with cocktail fruit.

My mom enrolled me and my younger siblings in Horace Mann Elementary. My fifth-grade teacher was a dark skin African-American woman. She said I was very smart and had a lot of potential the first time we met. I admired her intelligence and elegance.

My younger cousin was in the same class as me. I got into my first fight and it was with a Tongan girl. She was big and mean. She was trying to tell me to do something that I didn't want to do. My cousin told me to not let her push me around. So, I stood up from my seat and told her to leave me alone. She pushed me back down into my seat. I stood up again and began punching her. I don't know if my punches were connecting but I sure did feel hers. I had a headache after that fight and wished I never listened to my cousin.

My mom was diagnosed with diabetes, and she lost a lot of weight. She was not feeling well enough to attend my fifth-grade graduation. So, I stayed home with her instead of going to the graduation alone.

My older half-sister's friend came by and insisted I go. She said she would take me herself, but I told her I didn't have anything nice to wear. My mom said I could wear her black suede dress and a pair of black heels. My sister's friend applied some light makeup on my face and put my braids up into a hairstyle.

We walked to my elementary school and realized I was too late. The graduation celebration was over. I walked to my fifth-grade class and my teacher gave me my certificate for completing elementary and a bouquet. She said she was proud of me and believed I would do well in life.

One day I was sitting in the living room with my family when my mom received a phone call from a friend. Her friend said she had just seen my dad. My mom didn't believe her, so she picked up her phone and called the prison where my dad was supposed to be.

They stated my dad had been released a few months ago. We were all shocked. We were in disbelief and confused as to why we were just finding out and why my dad had not contacted us yet.

I decided to walk down to my dad's mom's house to get some answers. My siblings came along with me. We arrived at my grandmother's house, and I rang the doorbell. No one came to the door, so I rang it again, and again, and again. I knew someone was home because her car was still in the driveway. I decided to take it a step further to get a response. I grabbed the water hose, turned on the water, and stuck the water hose through my grandmother's basement window.

After a few minutes, my grandmother came to the door. She asked, "What the hell are you doing?!" I asked, "Where is my daddy? Why didn't you tell us he was out? Where is he?" She said, "I don't know what you are talking about, but your daddy is not here." I called her a liar, cursed her out, and continued to ask where my dad was.

A few minutes passed and my dad came to the door. I froze like I saw a ghost. I had not seen my dad in 6 years and suddenly, he appeared in the doorway asking why I was being so disrespectful. I did not respond. I turned around and ran home. My sister and brothers ran behind me.

When I got home, I told my mom,

Anne, and granny what happened. A few hours later there was a knock on the door. My mom opened it and it was my dad. He explained that he needed some time before he was ready to let us know he was home. He said it was hard to adjust after being released from prison. He said he needed some time before he was reunited with his family again. He also said he was in disbelief to hear the words that were coming out of my mouth. He could not believe how much I had grown and how disrespectful I was to his mother.

I wanted to apologize for my behavior. I wanted to hug him and let him know how sorry I was and how much I missed him. I was happy he was home, but something didn't feel right with this whole situation. So, I didn't say anything. I got up and went into my room.

A few days later I was at my granny's house, my mom's mom, and my papa came over. He asked me what happened recently. I acted like I had no clue about what he was talking about. He said, "Your grandmother called me and told me what you did. So, do you think you were right or wrong?" I replied, "Wrong." Then he asked, "Do you think you deserve a whooping?" I didn't want to lie but I also didn't want a whooping. So, to avoid making things worse, I said "Yes." He said, "Okay" and started taking off his belt.

I tried to get myself ready for this whooping. I told myself it wasn't going to hurt.

It was going to be quick and just get it over with.

He grabbed me by the hand, lifted his belt in the air, and brought it down quickly onto my butt. I jumped and screamed. I could not endure the sting.

He continued to lift the belt in the air and bring it down onto my butt. I screamed and ran all around the room trying to get away from him. I said, "That's enough Papa. That's enough." When he finished, he said, "This hurts me more than it hurts you."

I did not learn my lesson. A few days later, my mom called my dad's phone and heard my granny and Anne talking in the background. My dad must have answered the phone by accident because he did not say hello. My mom sat on the phone listening to their conversation and then she began to cry. She told me Anne and Daddy were sleeping together.

I became angry seeing my mom cry. My mom told me and my siblings to get dressed and put on our shoes. We walked to my granny's house and saw my dad out front laughing with Anne. My mom started to push him and curse him out. He began walking down the street, away from us, so we followed him. My siblings and I joined in the chaos and started cursing my dad out too.

People watched and asked why my dad

was letting us disrespect him like that. They said, "If those were my kids, I would beat their ass." My dad ran to his mom's house. So, we stopped following him and walked back home.

My dad came over to my mom's apartment the next day. He told my mom that she did not hear what she thought she heard. He said Anne was jealous of their relationship and she was trying to make my mom upset. He said Anne was trying to have sex with him, but he turned her down. My mom believed him, and they got back together.

CHAPTER 11 CALVIN SIMMONS

My mom and I stayed up late one night while she braided my hair for school the next day. It was going to be my first day of middle school. I was excited and nervous about starting the sixth grade.

I did not want to get bullied like I did in elementary school. That night I decided I was going to be tough and brave. I was not going to let anyone tease me or bully me. I was not going to let anyone disrespect me or hurt me in any type of way.

The next day came, and I was ready. I caught the bus to school and put on my mean mug, my "don't fuck with me" face.

A short Mexican girl walked up to me and asked if I was okay. I looked at her and thought, what is her deal? What is wrong with her? Can't she see that I'm mean? Can't she see that I don't want to be bothered? I replied, "Yes, I'm fine." Then she asked, "Do you want to be friends?" I was surprised. My plan did not work. At least not with this girl. Either I did not look mean enough, or she just was not scared. So, I replied "Yes."

I am grateful we met. I am grateful she started that conversation and became my best friend. She was a Gemini just like my mom and dad. She lived with her dad and two sisters. We spent a lot of time together. I enjoyed spending the night at her house. We watched novellas, ate Mexican food, and talked about the boys we liked.

I joined the school band and started to learn how to play the flute. We were getting ready for our first concert. I was so happy and excited. I invited my dad to attend. I was proud of myself and I wanted to share my joy and skill with my father.

I sat in my seat and watched as families strolled through the school doors. The auditorium started to get full, and I did not see my dad walk through the door yet.

I began to become very anxious and nervous. My stomach started to hurt. I thought he wasn't coming. Tears started to rise in my eyes, and I felt like something was stuck in my throat.

Then I saw him walk through the door. He was carrying roses in his hands. For the first time, a parent showed up for me. I was so happy to see him there.

My first school dance was in sixth grade. My friends and I danced together. I shook my head back and forth like I had dreads. I had a fun time. That was my last dance for a while.

I still tried to act tough in middle school as I went into the seventh grade. I had this mindset that I had to hurt others before they tried to hurt me. I ended up hurting people who did not deserve it. I became a bully.

My behavior caught up with me one day. There was a rumor going around that some girls were planning to jump me. So, the next day I brought a knife to school. I told a few people I had brought it to protect myself just in case they tried to jump on me.

The next day I came back to school without the knife. The school security guard came to my class and told me to get all my things and to follow them. She took me into an empty classroom and looked inside my backpack. Then she had me empty my pockets and patted me down. She asked, "Do you have a knife?" I said, "No." Then she asked, "Did you have one yesterday?" And I said, "Yes."

She took me to the office and the

principal told me I was getting expelled. I had

to leave the school and never return. I was so

devastated. I thought my life was over.

CHAPTER 12 FIRST BOYFRIEND

I did not go outside often. I mostly stayed in the apartment, cleaning, cooking, and taking care of my siblings and my mom.

One day my siblings asked me to go outside with them. At first, I said no but then I changed my mind. I decided it would be a good idea to keep an eye on them and see what they were up to.

We rode our bikes down the hill toward 47th and Bancroft. I saw a group of boys hanging outside in front of some apartments. One of the boys yelled, "Hey Mamie, come here." I stopped and looked at the group of boys for a few seconds. He waved his hand

and said, "Come here. I won't bite." And then he smiled and laughed.

I told my siblings to come with me to see what he wanted. We rode our bikes toward them, and he asked, "What is your name?" I said, "Nay Nay." He said, "How old are you?" I lied and said I was sixteen. I was twelve, but I looked mature for my age because my body was fully developed. He told me his name and said he was 19 years old. He wrote his number down on a piece of paper and gave it to me.

His friends were smoking weed and they passed it to him. He asked me if I wanted to hit it and I said no. He asked if I had ever tried it before and I replied, "No." He said, "Give it a try. You might like it." So, I took the blunt from his hand and tried to smoke it. His friends started yelling at me saying I was wasting the weed because I wasn't inhaling it. I passed the blunt back to him and told him I had to go. He said, "All right, make sure you call me later." I said, "Okay" and rode off with my sister and brothers.

I called him later that night and we talked on the phone for hours. I talked to him every day and night for the next few days. He asked me to come over to his place. I told him I wanted to, so we started making plans.

The day finally came, and I went to his apartment. He lived on 73rd and International in an apartment above a store. His room was painted red, green, and white. He had a

Mexican flag and a picture of Jesus hanging on the wall. There were red, green, and white candles throughout his room, and they smelled like peppermint.

I sat on his bed smiling and admiring him. Then his phone rang and at the other end of the phone was my mom. She asked, "Is my daughter with you?" He replied, "Who is this, and who is your daughter?" She said, "Her name is Nay Nay. She is only twelve years old. If she is with you, please send her home." He said, "Your daughter isn't with me." She said, "I found your number in her room. She is a minor. I will call the police and report statutory rape if you don't send her home now." He laughed and hung up the phone.

I did not consider the anguish my mom must have felt. I did not consider her stress or worries. I wanted someone to love me unconditionally and I thought he could be that person. I lost my virginity to him that night and I did not enjoy it. It was very painful.

The next day I woke up early and went home. I walked inside my apartment and my mom and dad were sitting on the couch in the living room. My mom jumped up and ran toward me. She started yelling, "Where the fuck have you been?!" I said, "I was out." She said, "I know you were out, but out where?" I didn't respond.

She asked, "Nay-Nay did you lose your virginity?" I said, "No." She said, "You are lying. Pull down your pants and let me see." I said, "No. That's weird." She said, "Do it now!" and then she started grabbing onto my pants, trying to pull them down. I grabbed her hands and pushed them away. I pulled away from her and ran outside down the back door stairs. I ran from 48th and Ygnacio to my granny's house on 57th and Bancroft.

My mom came down to my granny's house an hour later. We started arguing and I ran into the bathroom and locked the door. She grabbed a knife from the kitchen and started sliding it under the bathroom door. We were yelling back and forth at each other. She kicked in the door and started punching me. I started punching her back until Anne broke up the fight.

She walked back home, and I stayed at my granny's house for a few days. I went back home, and we got into another argument. I grabbed a knife and started pointing it at my chest. I started yelling, "It's all your fault! It's all your fault I'm like this. You don't love me. You didn't believe me. You didn't protect me. I don't want to be here anymore. I want to die." I kept poking myself in the chest and she called 911.

The paramedics took me to a mental hospital in Berkeley, CA. The doctors diagnosed me with 51/50. I started to believe I was truly crazy after I saw 51/50 next to my name. I finally became a crazy woman.

My mom and dad visited me at the mental hospital. We sat at a table quietly and then my mom said, "You were telling the truth huh? He did that to you?" I looked up at her and I started to cry. I said, "Yes, he did." Then she started to cry too. She said, "I'm so sorry Nay. Please forgive me." I forgave my mother that day. I stayed in the hospital for a total of three days and then I was released back to my mom and dad.

I continued to date my boyfriend. He eventually met my mom. She said she liked him, and he was very handsome. She still did not feel comfortable with me dating a 19-year-old boy. My dad did not like him at all. He did not want to meet him, and he did not want us to continue dating.

One day I came home late, and my dad asked, "Who do you think you are coming in here so late? Where have you been?" I said, "With my boyfriend." He started talking about how he didn't like him, he was too old for me, and a bad influence. My dad said, "You ask me for money for clothes, shoes, and your phone bill. You should be asking that nigga for money instead of me. You should date someone who can take care of you. Don't be fucking for free." His statements stuck with me throughout my life.

I began to get annoyed by him, so I said, "Why are you so worried about him? Do you want to date him or something? You keep

his name in your mouth." My dad got angry.
He balled up his fist and started punching me
in the legs. I tried to move away, and he
accidentally punched me in the ear. I ran into
my room and called 911. I told them my dad
had beaten me.

The police knocked on our door and
asked me and my dad to come outside. They
asked us what happened, and we both told
them our story. The officer looked at me and
said, "If you were my daughter, I would whoop
your ass too." He said, "Go back inside and go
to bed." And he told my dad to have a good
night. I could not believe the police did not
arrest my dad for child abuse.

The next few days I tried calling my

boyfriend, but he did not answer. So, I decided to go down the street to the place where I met him. One of his friends who lived there was standing out front. I asked him if he had seen or spoken to my boyfriend, and he said no. He asked if I could braid his hair and I told him yes. He grabbed some chairs, a comb, and some rubber bands. We sat out front while I braided his hair. I walked back home when I was done.

My boyfriend called me when I got home. He asked me where I had been. I told him I was at his friend's house looking for him. He said I should not have been there. That it was inappropriate and made him look bad. He broke up with me that day.

I apologized numerous times and tried to get back together with him, but he would not take me back. I went over to his apartment hoping we would get back together, but we just had sex and stayed broken up. The last time I saw him I was 15 years old. He came over to my mom's apartment drunk. He apologized for the way he treated me and then he left. That same night he was arrested and went to prison.

CHAPTER 13 CDS

My mom enrolled me in a continuation school in Oakland Hills. I walked from 48th and Ygnacio to High St. to catch the bus to the school. I stood at the bus stop with other students who were waiting for the same bus. I stood there quietly and kept to myself.

The bus finally came, and we all got on board. We rode up to Community Day School (CDS). The school was small and divided into two sections. One side was the middle school and the other was the high school. The schools had two to three classrooms and about 10 to 20 students on each side.

I started attending the eighth grade at

CDS. My math teacher was a Black man with dreads. I enjoyed his class. I enjoyed solving problems and getting the math problems right.

My English teacher was an Asian American woman. She was fun. She spoke slang, let us listen to music, and recite poetry. Our computer, history, and science classes were with the same teachers.

I met a new friend. She was another Gemini. She was light-skinned and skinny with long black hair. She had a lot of brothers and sisters. We spent a lot of time together. I enjoyed hanging out with her and her family. Again, I felt like I found a second family.

One day, I got on the bus heading

home from school and a boy approached me. He started flirting with me and gave me the nickname Glossy because I had so much lip gloss on my lips. He was a student on the high school side and he was in a relationship.

His girlfriend started arguing with me the next day as we were getting on the bus. She stood up and I thought she was about to start fighting. So, I stood up too and began to punch her. The bus driver told us to get off the bus and go back home. The school called my mom and told her they suspended me for fighting on the school bus.

After my suspension, I walked to the bus stop to head back to school. I got on the bus, and the boy said, "You fought her over me?" And I replied, "Yes." We continued to talk, and I became his girlfriend.

We talked on the phone a lot and started making plans for my birthday that was coming up. He wanted to do something special for me. So, he asked me to come to his house.

I rode the bus from East Oakland to West Oakland. I got off on 7th St. and walked toward his house. I knocked on the door and he opened it. He said, "Hi Glossy, come in." I said, "Hi" and walked through the door. We walked down the hall, and into his room.

He handed me some balloons and a small box. In the box was a silver necklace. He took the necklace out of the box and put it around my neck. He turned on some music and started singing Ride or Die by Go Dav. He said, "For me, you'll ride or die, I look in your eyes. I'll see the sunset tonight forever. For me you'll ride or die, I look in your eyes. I'll see the sun she sets, tonight, forever, my baby." I was amazed by his voice. He was a great singer. I fell in love with that song, and I fell for him. I never had anyone sing to me before. I was his Glossy, his ride-or-die. We danced slowly and then he started to take off my clothes. We had sex and he asked if he was my first. I lied and said yes. Again, I did not enjoy having sex. It still was painful.

We got dressed, took a shower, and went outside to hang out with his sister and friends. We rode the bus to the movies and then went back to his house for some cake and ice cream. I enjoyed my birthday, and I enjoyed spending time with him.

It was another night when my mom was worried. She found his number in my room and called him multiple times looking for me. We ignored her calls and the next day I went home.

A few days later I got on the bus heading to school, and people were saying my boyfriend had gotten shot. I called his phone, but he did not answer. The next day people were saying they had conversations with him. He told them he was doing okay and recovering at home. People were surprised that

I had not talked to him yet. I was worried and embarrassed.

I continued calling his phone, but he still did not answer. I became angry. I did not understand why he was answering other people's calls and not mine. So, I told people to tell him it was over the next time they spoke to him.

A few weeks later he got on the bus heading to school. I said, "What happened? Why weren't you answering my calls?" He said, "I was hurting. I was in a lot of pain, and I did not want you to see me that way." I said, "That's not fair. Other people were able to talk to you and visit you, but I was not. I was supposed to be your girl. Your ride or die." He said, "Well you aren't my ride or die. You broke

up with me after I got shot." I said, "I broke

up with you because of the silent treatment." I

wrote a poem after our conversation, and I

wrote:

I Miss You

I cannot let you go
You are still in my heart
I love you even more
Since we are torn apart
I miss you
Hoping we can be together soon
I cannot stand us being like this
not talking and all this shit
You're making me go crazy
I fucking miss you, baby,
But you made me let you go
Wouldn't answer my phone calls
You know that was wrong
But here I am
Still in the fall
All I do is cry
Wishing things were different
Wishing you were by my side
My feelings I cannot hide

And that is not going to change
I still want you to claim
Not starting more commotion
Just you as my main
When I call you, I do not want trouble
Just to be cool
But when I think about how you treated me
I want to act like a fool
That's one thing I hate about us on earth
We cannot understand each other
Without someone getting hurt

A few weeks later I started dating

someone else. He was a Mexican boy with long

hair. We attended the same classes on the

middle school side. We went on a field trip to

the ice-skating rink. It was my first time going.

I didn't know how to skate, so he taught me.

He held my hand and we skated around and

around the rink until it was time to go.

One day I was feeling overwhelmed. I

felt like I needed someone to talk to. So, I

walked into the school's office to speak to the school counselor. My heart was heavy, and my thoughts were spiraling out of control.

I told the counselor I was thinking about committing suicide. I told her I was very unhappy. I said I felt sad and alone. Things weren't good at home. My mom was abusing my sister and it was taking a toll on my mental health. I didn't know how to stop it or how to help my little sister. I told her my mom was never loving toward my sister. She did not change her or feed her when she was a baby. My mom would cook dinner and not fix my sister a plate. My granny and I had to steal food out of the kitchen, sneak it into my room, and feed my sister. I caught my sister drinking out of the toilet once because she was so thirsty. My mom would beat her and tell her she was ugly. My mom said she did not love her or want her.

My therapist called child protective services. I was sent back to the mental hospital and my sister was picked up from Frick middle school and placed into a foster home. I didn't want my sister to go into the foster care system.

Anne's kids had gotten placed into foster care, and we heard some terrible stories. They said kids were being molested, raped, and abused. It was sad and scary to be taken out of one home and placed in another where things were the same or much worse.

I didn't want my sister to go through that. I was worried about her. I was so upset with myself for opening my mouth. Once again, I wished I didn't say anything. I thought if something bad happened to her while she was in foster care, it would be my fault.

CHAPTER 14 FOSTER CARE

My sister and an old white man picked me up from the mental hospital when I was released. She said he was our foster parent and she had been staying with him, his wife, and some other foster children. We got in the car and drove to Sacramento.

We stayed with this family for a few months. They seemed nice at first but then things got weird. They wouldn't let us call home. We asked to call our mom and they said no. They said, "If your mother wanted to talk to you then she would call."

So, we waited for her call but we never received one. My sister became discouraged.

She said, "Mama doesn't love us or want us anymore. We are never going back home." I tried to comfort her. I told her, "I don't think that is true. We are going back home one day. Regardless of what happens, she will always have me. We will always be together."

I took one of my bracelets from my wrist, bent it until it broke, took the pointy part, and carved her name into my arm. I was a bit extreme. I thought I needed to show my love for others passionately. Why not carve my sister's name in my arm to show her how much love I have for her? And I liked carving things into my arm. I liked the pain.

Later we found out that the foster parents were unplugging the phone and that was why we didn't receive any calls from my mom. We told our social worker, and she placed us into another foster home.

We temporarily lived with a Black woman and three black foster girls. We stayed with them for a few days while our social worker looked for a permanent foster home for us to live in.

We moved to a foster home in Vallejo, CA. We lived with a middle-aged Black woman who ran a daycare center and two teenage Black girls who were in foster care.

We helped the foster mom with her daycare center. We watched the kids, warmed up spaghetti, and served it. We watched

Barney and played games with the kids.

I was enrolled in middle school and one day I made a stupid decision and decided I wanted to get the attention of the cool kids. So, I started a fight with a girl I did not know and who didn't do anything to me. I picked her randomly. I got off the bus at her stop and followed her down the street. I grabbed her by the hair and swung her around. She fell to the ground, and I grabbed her by the hair and dragged her face through the concrete.

The next day I was called into the principal's office and the girl I hurt was in there too. The principal asked me what happened, and I told her what I had done. The girl started to cry, and she said, "I wanted to be a model when I grew up and now my dream is over. You destroyed my face and my dream." The principal told her that her face would heal, and she would still be able to pursue her dream. She told the girl she was free to leave, and she told me to stay.

After the girl left, the principal asked me why I did it. I said, "I don't know. I just wanted to feel something besides sadness and anger. I wanted to get the attention of the cool kids." She said your life is your fault. I immediately felt like she was wrong. I started to think about all the terrible things that happened to me and said it was not my fault and she was wrong.

I believe she meant, "You get to choose

how you react to situations. You get to choose what you do after. You chose to hurt someone because you were hurt. You made a bad choice and that is your fault."

I regret what I did. I was a bully and I hurt her to get other's attention. I thought what I was doing was cool and funny, but I was wrong. I believe you should fight when you have to defend yourself. But I didn't have to defend myself. I didn't have a good reason to put my hands on her. She didn't do anything to me. She was a sweet and kind person. I chose to take all my anger out on her for nothing. She did not deserve the pain I caused. Bullying is wrong. I am sorry for what I did. It was wrong.

When you're young you may think it is cool and funny to hurt others, but when you get older you will regret it all. People deserve to feel safe. People deserve to go to school and make it back home safe. I have children now and I would be so hurt if someone did what I did to her or worse.

My foster mom picked me up from school and we drove home. I went into my room and stayed there until my sister came home from school. I told her we were leaving. We were going back home to our old life. We packed a small bag and went down the street to a neighbor's house. The boys from our school lived there. Their parents weren't home, but they let us come in anyway.

I called my boyfriend from CDS and told him my plan. He said he would try to find a ride for us to get back to Oakland. The day grew dark, and no one came. We spent the night at the boys' house and went back to the foster mom's house the next day.

The foster mom was fed up with my behavior. She called our social worker and told her what happened. The social worker came and picked us up and took us to another placement. A few days later my mom was granted custody of me and my sister. We went back home.

Shortly after going back home, my sister and brothers went to some kid's house they knew from school and took some things that belonged to their mom. The police came to our apartment and arrested my sister. She was sent to juvenile hall. She was diagnosed with bipolar disorder and placed on medication while she was there. My mom did not go to her court hearings or try to get her back. From that point on my sister was a ward of the State. She was in and out of group homes and started prostituting. I hated that life for her. She felt so unloved and unwanted.

Our social worker assigned me a therapist and got me into a mentor program. My therapist did a weekly home visit and made me an appointment with a psychiatrist. The psychiatrist prescribed me antidepressants.

My mentor was a Korean woman. She

was very caring, kind, and sweet. She took me to a coffee shop the first time we met. I had never been inside one before. I loved the atmosphere. I loved the smell of coffee roasting, and seeing people reading books, working on their computers, and socializing.

She bought me my first iPod and books to read. She encouraged me to do well in school. She took me to a lot of cool places I had never been to before. We went to a miniature golf course, Six Flags, and High Hill. We went to the movies, watched live plays, and to the nail salon. She invited me over to her house to watch movies and have dinner. She would cook my favorite meal, shrimp with rice. I enjoyed the time we shared.

Black History Month came around and I

drafted a poem. I wrote:

Society Changes

This world is so crazy
Crazier than before
We, youngstas, act so lazy
Not taking advantage of what's ours
Just acting like fools
Not using our minds as tools
The things we need
We got from our elders
They got mistreated and beat
They truly did suffer
We do not give them half
the respect they deserve
Most of us think about love and sex
Our shapes and curves
Throwing up turfs and clicks
Acting really dumb and sick
Dying over these streets
And there's no winner
We are all getting beat
Because we don't stick together
So, how are we going to succeed
MLK died for us
He died for freedom and love
But we keep acting like rips
And wanting to be tricks

Aren't you getting sick
Of the pain, you put yourself through
This is all a test
So, what are you going to do?
At least try to do your best
Would you really die for your turf?
Drinking and smoking may feel good
But in the end doesn't it hurt?
Let me tell you my story
All about my pain and worries
Being molested at seven
Becoming a Christian
And wanting to go to heaven
People believed I did things for attention
Started to claim my turf so hard
Even in my arms, it was carved
I was not thinking of the right things
Throwing away all my dreams
Blaming others for my mistakes
Believed my life was messed up
Because all people did was hate
I started to realize
I had a lot to change
With the one who was always by my side
Who helped me through my crazy rides
I did not want my siblings
to follow my wrong steps
So, I took the right turn and led
It is not easy to stop
What you're used to doing
I am still in the struggle
But soon I will be on top of all my troubles

Like they say
If you want a better life
You must learn from your mistakes
They made history and we can too
If we just believe in what we can do
Let us remember all the things
they went through
Not only for African Americans
But for all races too
We all have gifts, so use them
Mine is writing poems
Turning words into beautiful songs
We all need to hold on and stay strong
Open our eyes and realize
We make life seem like fire
And the fire constantly seems to get higher
Do you not want to make history?
Doing good things for all our needs
All you must do is believe
Dwell on my rhymes
Because every month is history month
Time to use our minds and give sunshine

My mom and dad did not attend my

eighth-grade graduation, but my dad's mom

showed up. She came with my dad's sister, my

cousin, and my niece. My grandmother

expressed how proud she was of me and how

she hoped I would continue to do well in

school. I wrote another poem and recited it at

my eighth-grade graduation.

A Good Citizen

What if we wrote a declaration
Of all the right things
Excluding the wrong laws
So, we will not have a reason to fight
We all can be an inspiring person
A good one making a good change
Working hard to eliminate
Things that are making us insane
Letting people know that we understand
Everything they are going through.
Letting them know that we have open hands
And all their problems will be better soon
Accelerate every step
To make a beautiful protest
We have big dreams that we will complete
Have the young and old lookup
And want to be like you and me
We can all succeed

CHAPTER 15 THE HOOD

I got my first job at 15. I started working as an after-school tutor at an elementary school for the East Bay Area Asian Youth Center (EBAYC). My mom and granny were so proud of me. They took pictures of me holding my first paycheck. I worked there for a few months.

While working there I started smoking weed and drinking alcohol. One night, I went to 71st Ave with my cousin to hang out with some people she knew. 71st was known as the hood in my family. It was the area my parents and grandparents lived and grew up in. It was the area where my dad sold drugs, and my mom and dad were known as Bonnie and

Clyde.

People I had never seen before walked up to me and said, "I know your mama and daddy". They told me crazy stories about my parents. I was surprised by how so many people knew them and showed respect for them.

My cousin smoked weed and I did not at the time. She tried to get me to smoke but I turned it down. So, she blew it in my face to get me a contact high.

One day I gave in. I asked her to hit the blunt. I put the blunt between my fingers, inhaled, and then started to cough. She laughed and called me a rookie. I gave it a few more tries and then I was high. I did not like the feeling. I felt paranoid. I felt scared. I wanted to go home and get into bed. I wanted to be in a safe place and around people I trusted.

A few days later I decided to give marijuana another try. I bought two dime bags from some guys who lived down the street from my mom's apartment. I bought a Swisher from the liquor store and walked back home.

I went into my room and started breaking down the weed with my nails. I placed the weed into the swisher and rolled it up. I licked the opening to make sure it would stick and stay close. I walked out of my room and out the back door onto our back stairs. I sat down, took out a lighter, and fired up the

blunt. I inhaled, exhaled, and then coughed. I

gave it a few more tries and then I put the

blunt out on the steps.

I walked back into the house and went

to my room. I did not feel paranoid or scared

this time. I felt happy. I thought about things

that made me happy and feel good.

I walked into my brothers' room and

asked if they wanted to play Grand Theft Auto.

They said yes and turned on the TV and the

PlayStation. I thought everything was funny.

They asked why was I laughing so much. I

said I was happy and having fun. I made this a

routine. I would smoke weed, play video

games with my little brothers, and then cook

us something to eat because I had munchies.

I started hanging out with my cousin again and some other kids she knew on 71st. They all sold weed and I decided I wanted to too. I bought some weed and baggies for the first time and took everything home to bag it up. I recall sitting in the living room with my mom and dad while I bagged up the weed. I told my parents about the people I ran into in the hood and the stories they told me about them. For the first time in a long time, we were talking and laughing together. I was finally on the same level. We had something to talk about that they could relate to. I wanted so badly to have a close relationship with them. I wanted them to praise me like they praised the other kids in our family who sold drugs, committed robberies, and engaged in fights.

One day I stood on the corner of 71st Ave while reading a book and trying to sell weed. My papa caught me and said, "Girl what are you doing? You don't belong out here. Why are you trying to be like other people? You look silly. Over here reading books and trying to sell weed. Take your butt home." I didn't go home. I walked down the street to my boyfriend's house. I started dating a boy who lived in the neighborhood.

I loved being in the hood. I loved hanging out with my favorite cousin, our friends, and my boyfriend. I became so infatuated with the lifestyle that I carved 7100 into my arm. I associated love with pain. I had to show how much I loved something by hurting myself. It was weird.

I started off drinking and smoking weed, and then I took it up a notch and bought some ecstasy. I bought it from a guy my cousin and friends knew. It was a rainy and cold night I took it and felt the effects 30 minutes later. My eyes became red and my pupils dilated. I started to grind my teeth and shiver from the coldness.

I became angry because I was so cold. I wanted to punch something or somebody. I wanted to cause some trouble, do something exciting, start a fight. I felt invincible. I felt so strong and brave. I felt all these things I never felt before and I liked these feelings. I wanted to feel these things more, so I started taking ecstasy every day. And then I started to lose a lot of weight but I didn't care. I just wanted to keep feeling good from getting high.

Instead of going to work as a tutor, I stayed in the hood, selling drugs, getting high and drunk, and hanging out with my boyfriend, my cousin, and friends.

Then I became very depressed and suicidal. I decided to take all my depression medication and any other pills I could find around the house. I laid on the couch and waited to die.

My papa showed up at my mom's

house. He knocked on the door a few times but I would not get up to open it. My brother walked into the living room and opened the door for him. My papa walked in and saw me lying on the couch.

He asked what was wrong with me and why I did not open the door. I said, "I'm waiting to die." He picked me up and walked me to his car. He drove me to the hospital and told the nurses and doctor something was wrong with me.

They asked me if I had taken anything, and I told them I had taken a lot of pills. They brought me a charcoal drink and had me drink it. I started vomiting a few minutes later. They sent me to a mental hospital for my safety.

My papa came to visit me and I was so angry with him. I started to cry and I asked him why did he do that. Why did he take me to the hospital? I said, "I wanted to die. I wanted to be free of this world. Free from this pain and suffering. I do not understand why God created me. I do not know my purpose."

He said, "I did it because I love you and because God loves you. God created you for a reason. I know you are hurting just like so many other people in this world. I understand you do not know your purpose or why God created you, but one day you will, and one day you will be grateful I took you to the hospital." And he was right. I am so grateful my papa saved me. I am so grateful to be alive.

CHAPTER 16 TOXIC

On April 16, 2009, I was 16 years old riding the bus when a boy sat next to me. He said I was very pretty and asked for my number, so I gave it to him before hopping off the bus.

Later that night he called me, and we spoke on the phone for hours. We discovered we both were waiting to attend Treasure Island Job Corps. My papa had taken me to the Job Corp's orientation a few months before. We filled out the paperwork and were waiting to hear back from them about my start date.

The boy and I continued to talk on the phone and hang out with each other until he started Job Corps. I was sad when he started because I wanted us to start together. Two weeks passed and I finally received the phone call with my start date. I started Job Corps on June 1, 2009.

I was so anxious and excited. I wanted to see him so badly. June 1st came, and my papa dropped me off with my luggage. I stood out front with some other kids who were starting the same day as me. We walked inside the building and checked in with Security. A woman came by and guided us through the campus. Then I saw him. He was outside with a few other kids. I waved excitedly at him. He smiled and waved back.

Attending Job Corps was a wonderful

experience. Monday through Friday we would wake up at 6 am to get ready for school. We walked out of the dorms and met each other outside by a bench. We walked hand in hand to the cafeteria, got in line to get our breakfast, and we sat at a table to eat together.

We cleaned off our trays, put them up, and walked outside to find a quiet place to sit. We talked, hugged, and kissed before going to class. Half of the day we attended high school and the other half we attended trade school. I took office administration, and he took carpentry.

After class, we walked back to the dorms. He went to his dorm room, and I walked to mine. We took a shower and got ready for dinner. We met outside by the bench again and walked to the cafeteria. We ate dinner together and walked back to the dorms.

There was a game room on the first floor. We played pool, spades, and dominoes. On movie night, we grabbed snacks and watched movies together. Sometimes we went on dates in San Francisco. We bought puff pastries, toured the city, and went to the movies.

One night we went to the theater to watch the movie 2012. I wore a black Dereon dress and some black heels. He wore black slacks and a white-collar shirt. We waited up till midnight to watch the premier. The movie was scary. I thought we were really going to die in 2012.

We graduated from Job Corps with our high school diplomas and trade certificates. I was selected to speak at my high school graduation, and I recited a poem.

My mom was so excited that I was graduating. She bought me a dress and a pair of heels. She attended my graduation with my younger brothers. My dad's mother and sister came to my graduation too.

After graduation, I had the option to stay on campus while attending college or go back home. I chose to go back home to help my mom. She was still losing a lot of weight and struggling with her diabetes.

I moved back home and enrolled in
Laney College. On the first day, I took the bus
to the college, walked onto the campus, and
waited by the classroom door for the instructor
to arrive. The teacher walked up, unlocked the
door, and stood by while all the students
walked inside. I took a seat near the front.

The instructor introduced themself and
started discussing the syllabus, books, and
supplies we needed. I started to feel
intimidated. I did not understand what she was
saying or referring to. I felt lost and afraid. I
felt too ashamed to ask questions. I did not
return to class.

I decided I would get a job instead of going to school. So, I started applying for office jobs, but I was unsuccessful in obtaining one. My granny had gotten approved for an in-home caretaker, and she decided she wanted me to be the person who would take care of her and get paid for it. So, we went to Eastmont Mall to attend the orientation and submit the paperwork.

I started taking care of my granny and had to wait a few weeks before receiving my first check. In the meantime, I knew I wanted to buy a car. So, I studied, took the written test, and passed. My boyfriend gave me driving lessons in an empty parking lot by the Coliseum Bart station. I scheduled my driving test and passed that too. I received my first paycheck from IHSS, and I was ready to buy my first car. My dad and I caught the bus to check out a car and test drive it. I bought a white two-door Thunderbird LX.

My boyfriend and I had been dating for 2 years, and I wanted to spend every second with him. One day while hanging out together, he decided he was going to go hang out with some of his cousins and friends. I was so clinging; I gave him an ultimatum. I said, "You either stay with me or I will go hang out with someone who wants to spend time with me." He said, "Go ahead." And he left.

I called my ex-boyfriend from West Oakland. I got on the bus, went to his house, and cheated on my boyfriend. I called my boyfriend on my way home and told him what I had done. He broke up with me.

For the next few weeks, I tried to get back with him, but he would not take me back. I told him how sorry I was, and that I would never do it again, but he refused to give me another chance.

After a few weeks of trying, he finally took me back. We were doing good for a while. Then, I started drinking more and causing arguments. One day we were in my room drinking alcohol and watching T.V. I started getting irritated and wanted him to leave. I cursed him out and told him he had to go. He walked out the front door and I followed behind him. I was screaming and shouting. I was throwing my hands in the air and my neighbors were watching. I embarrassed myself and him.

Sometimes, I wish I never tried to get back with him because he deserved better. He did not deserve to be treated the way I treated him. I was so immature and toxic. I continued to cheat on him, and he took me back every time. He loved me even though my actions showed that I did not love him back.

I was 18 years old when I asked my boyfriend to have a baby with me. He said no because we were too young. He said, "We just graduated high school and we should focus on enjoying our lives and improving ourselves."

He was right but I still wanted a baby. His mom heard our conversation and told him to break up with me because I was crazy.

Shortly after, I became pregnant, and he was there right by my side. His family was so upset when we told them the news. They came to my mom's apartment wanting to fight me. They stood on our stairs cursing me out while my mom and dad stood in front of me, trying to protect me. After a while, they left.

I turned 20 weeks pregnant, and my mom, boyfriend, and I went to the doctor to find out if we were having a boy or a girl. We were all hoping for a boy, and we got what we wanted.

My mom moved from 47th and Ygnacio to 52nd and Ygnacio during my pregnancy. The new apartment was bigger. It had three bedrooms and two bathrooms. It also had a side yard. We packed up our things and moved to the new apartment. The front door was red, and the landlord told us red doors meant good luck. After living there for a while, my mom felt like the landlord lied about the red door and good luck. She said, "Good luck my ass."

One day my boyfriend and I were spending time together in my new room. I went through his phone and became upset when I saw he was talking to other girls on Facebook. I told him to leave but he wouldn't go. I told him that I was going to my brother's court hearing with my mom, and no one was going to be home, so he had to leave, but he still wouldn't go. So, I told my mom and she put him out.

My mom and I walked outside to get in the car and my boyfriend ran toward me and pushed me to the ground. I fell on my side, and I stayed on the ground for a few minutes holding my belly.

My mom started to punch him and curse him out. She called the police, and they came and arrested him. The paramedics came too and drove me to the hospital. The doctors and nurses checked on me and the baby and stated we were okay to be discharged.

My boyfriend got out of jail a few weeks later and we got back together. He got himself a job at a bakery factory and he bought me an engagement ring. We thought getting married would fix all our problems.

My mom used to get upset when my dad wanted to hang out with his friends. She sliced his tires and put sugar in his gas tank. She even drove me and my older cousin to my grandmother's house and asked my cousin to break the windows of my dad's car. My cousin did it and she cut her hand badly.

One day my mom and dad got into an argument and he picked her up and threw her onto the ground. She broke her ankle and went to the hospital to get it fixed but it never healed. The doctors discovered gangrene in her ankle. They suggested surgery but she didn't want them to amputate her foot. My mom was in and out of the hospital a lot because of her diabetes and ankle.

One day my mom and I were driving in her car while I was pregnant and she saw my dad crossing the street. He was coming from the liquor store. She was mad at him so she jumped on the curb and tried to run him over. She ran over his foot and drove back home. The police came to our door and arrested her. I couldn't believe my dad called the police on my mom. I was shocked to see her get arrested.

My siblings and I called my dad's mom's

house looking for my dad so we could talk to him. We wanted to ask him not to press charges against my mom. She was sick. She had diabetes, a broken ankle, and gangrene in her leg. My grandmother, aunt, and older sister got annoyed and told us to stop calling her house. My younger sister cursed them all out and said she would come down there and beat them up. My grandmother got a restraining order on her. My dad didn't press charges so, my mom was released within a few days.

I was 42 weeks old and was scheduled to get induced. My boyfriend, his mom, my mom, granny, sister, youngest brother, and best friend were all at the hospital with me on my scheduled induction day. My water broke before they could start the induction.

I was fully dilated a few hours after my water broke. January 14th is when I became a mother. I was 19 years old. I wish I would have waited to have my first child. I wish I would have prepared myself mentally, spiritually, and financially. I was still young and I was not ready to be a mom yet but I am grateful to have him.

Pushing him out was so hard. He was stuck for a while. When he finally came out, he was not breathing and had the umbilical cord wrapped around his neck. The doctors did everything they could and I heard my son cry. They placed him on my chest and I held him close. My mom placed her head onto mine and

I felt her tears drop from her face and roll down mine. I was not ready to be a mom but I knew our son was a blessing from God.

His dad picked him up from my chest and held him in his arms. He smiled ear to ear as he gazed at our baby boy. We were young and immature, but we felt so blessed to have been able to create a beautiful little life.

My mom held him next. She coddled him and stared at him with admiration. My granny was next and she did the same. She gave him a nickname. My granny came up with the most ridiculous nicknames. She gave him the nickname Mailman because she said he looked like one.

My youngest brother held him after my granny. He sat down and started to cry. My mom, granny and I were in awe watching that moment. This was his first time holding a baby, an innocent and precious life. He said he was shocked that he started to cry but he couldn't hold back his emotions.

Next, my sister and best friend held our son. My sister coddled him in her arms and stared at him with admiration. My best friend did the same and became his Godmother.

Our son was placed back into my arms and I started to sing to him. I said, "Mommy's baby, Mommy's baby, I love you, I love you. Mommy loves her baby. Mommy loves her baby. Yes, I do. Yes, I do." I sang it over and over again. I couldn't believe I finally got what I always wanted, a baby. Someone I believed would love me unconditionally.

The next day my boyfriend and I got into an argument. He threw my phone at me and left the hospital. Our son and I were discharged from the hospital a few days later but I had to return because I had a UTI and gallstones. I asked my boyfriend if he could go to the hospital with me to help me with our son, but he said no. We stayed at the hospital until I felt better. We were discharged and went back home to my mom. My boyfriend started to come over to my mom's apartment to spend time with our son.

One day I planned to go to the movies

with my cousins and my boyfriend said he would come over and keep our son while I went out. He came over and said he changed his mind and didn't want me to go. I told him I had already made plans. He said he wasn't going to watch our son and left. So, I didn't go to the movies. I ended up staying home with our son.

Another day I went through his phone and saw he was talking to other girls again. I had gotten upset and told him it was over. We started arguing and my mom told him he had to leave. He would not go, so she dragged him out and locked the door.

He started knocking on the door. I sat our son into his swing which was a few feet away from my bedroom window. My boyfriend broke my window and glass shattered all over the floor and our son. My boyfriend hopped through the window and grabbed our son. I grabbed him too and we started pulling him back and forth.

My mom came in and saw the commotion. She saw blood on the walls, the floor, and our son's pajamas. My mom freaked out and thought the blood was mine or our baby, but it wasn't. It was from my boyfriend's hand when he broke the window. My mom started to punch my boyfriend and then she called 911.

The police came and arrested my boyfriend. My mom suggested I get a restraining order. The police told me I had to go to the clerk's office to get a restraining order. My mom took me the next day. The process was quick and easy. I had gotten a temporary restraining order that lasted a few weeks and then I received a 5-year restraining order. We continued to break up and get back together.

I always felt like I didn't have the hustling genes in me that my family had, but one day I realized I just needed motivation. Our son's first Christmas was coming up and I wanted to make sure it was a nice one. I applied for jobs and finally obtained one. My cousin and I both started working for a scammy company. They had us selling knockoff perfume and cologne. They convinced us if we sold enough then we would get a high reward. So, we thought we might as well give it a try since we were broke. We were earning pennies from each sale. We were not feeling the job so we took the product they gave us and sold it on our own time and kept all the profit.

One day, I got up early and went to the gas station on 73rd Ave and Hegenberger Rd. I hustled my butt off that day selling perfume and cologne. I even asked for donations if people told me no, they were not interested in purchasing perfume or cologne. I made enough money to buy our son a pair of Jordans, some clothes, toys, and coloring books. I was so proud of myself for being able to pull it off.

My boyfriend got another job at a restaurant, and he put in a good word for me to get a job there too. We got our first apartment together on 35th Ave in East Oakland. We were excited and happy. We thought everything would be better, but they weren't.

We still argued a lot and he could not forgive me for the past things I did. He kept bringing them up and I didn't want to talk about it. I apologized so many times, but he was still hurt. Every time we argued I wanted him to leave but he wouldn't go so I called the police and he got arrested for violating the restraining order.

I met a girl through my sister while my son's father was in jail. We started dating and she moved into the apartment with me. My boyfriend was incredibly sad when he found out about it.

I wish I would have known then what I know now. I wish I would have treated him better. I wish I wasn't so toxic and loved him how he deserved to be loved. I cannot take back the things I said and did but I am so sorry for all of it.

CHAPTER 17 NEGATIVITY

My granny was known as a crazy woman. My mom was known as a crazy woman too. I started to follow in their footsteps and I became a crazy woman too.

I used to feed negativity to myself daily. I told myself over and over again I was crazy just like my dysfunctional family. I was crazy like my granny, mom, Anne, and cousins.

I said mean things to myself like I was dumb, ugly, and foolish. I said I would never be with someone who would love me unconditionally. I didn't deserve to be loved. I was a horrible person and I deserved to die. I was a mess. I was toxic. I thought I would never change. I told myself it would be best to just kill myself and I was a waste to the world.

Sometimes I enjoyed living in pain, being depressed, and being stressed. It was all I knew. I carved things in my arms because I liked the pain. I started to get tattoos because I liked the pain. I started to drink, smoke weed, and take ecstasy because it made me feel good for a little while. I thought I needed external things to make me happy. I thought I needed others' love and attention to be happy.

I recall throwing myself a party on my 18th birthday. I invited people I knew and some people I didn't know. I just wanted to make sure people showed up. I bought food, drinks, alcohol, and a cake. I took some ecstasy pills and danced with my boyfriend and sister. I was enjoying my birthday party until my dad's best friend's daughter tried to have sex with my youngest brother. She was nineteen and he was only eleven years old. So, I told her she had to leave. We got into an argument, and I chased her around the apartment building trying to fight her. My brother said I was a hater because I got in his way.

One day I was hanging out with my cousins and we were driving in a car with some guys they knew. We were drinking, smoking, and popping pills. I started feeling invincible again. I began to argue with the guys. One of them pulled out a gun on me and said he would shoot me if I didn't shut up. But I didn't shut up. I kept yelling and cursing them out. My cousins begged me to be quiet before I got myself killed. I said, "He ain't go do shit!" My cousins said, "Drop us off right here. She is tripping". The guys dropped us off on 73rd and Foothill. We waited for a bus and went back home.

Another time I was driving and swerving in my car. I almost ran into another car. The guy driving in that car pulled up on the side of me and said, "Hey you almost hit my car back there and if you did, I would have popped you." He held his gun up and pointed it at me.

One night, I went to San Francisco with some girls I met in my neighborhood to sell crack cocaine. They told me I had to hold the baggies in my mouth under my tongue and when I ran out, I could go get more from a guy they knew.

One of the bags ripped open under my tongue and I started to taste the drugs. I spit it all out and told them I was done and wanted to go home. They said okay but I had to find my way back. I called a friend and they picked me up. It was like 2 a.m. when I got home. I knocked on the door and my mom let me. I asked if I could lie in bed with her and she said yes.

I cried because I was so high but also because I felt so bad. I felt like a terrible daughter. I caused a lot of stress for my mom.

She didn't deserve the stress I put her through. I was always putting my life in danger and she was always worried about me. She laid next to me and held me while I cried. She kissed my forehead and said, "Nay, it's okay. You are home and you are safe."

Drugs and alcohol helped me feel good sometimes. Sometimes it helped me escape the chaos of the world. It made me feel strong, brave, courageous, and invincible. Sometimes it made me feel paranoid, scared, and out of my mind. Sometimes I took a lot of pills and I could have overdosed. Sometimes I felt more suicidal than I was before. Sometimes I drank so much that I passed out and forgot everything that happened the previous day.

Drugs and alcohol led me down some dangerous paths. Drinking and doing drugs may feel good but in the end, it really did hurt. It helped for a little while but when the high went away my problems stayed. They were still there waiting for me to make the right move.

I am so grateful to God that I did not die every time I took a risk with my life.

CHAPTER 18 DEATH

Tired Heart

While her mind raced
Her heart slowed down
Her mind was on speed
While her heart took a bow
It gave up on all it had to do
It gave up on loving me and you
Her mind told her to keep going
But her heart said it was too tired of showing
Showing up for her
Showing up for me and you
Her heart said it was through
Her mind said one more second, minute, hour
But her heart said No, I am just too tired

On September 6, 2013, I received a call from my mom. She said she wanted me and my son to spend the weekend with her. I told her my girlfriend and I had plans to go out of town, but that was not true. Instead, we stayed in North Oakland at my girlfriend's mom's apartment.

Later that night I received a call from my youngest brother. He said, "Nay Nay, mama is gone." I said, "What do you mean? Gone where?" He said, "She died." I said, "Stop playing with me." He said, "I'm serious." I said, "Put the paramedics on the phone." A few seconds passed and a man got on the phone. He said, "We received a 911 call that a woman was not breathing. We tried to resuscitate her, but we were unsuccessful."

I started to scream and cry. I felt like my brain was on fire and my heart was being squeezed. I cried and screamed for a few minutes. My son, girlfriend, and her family surrounded me. They were all concerned and asked what was wrong, but I could not speak.

After a while of screaming and crying, I finally said, "I need to go home. I need to go to my mom. They said she died." My girlfriend's mom said, "Okay, I will take you." My son stayed with my girlfriend's brothers and girlfriend, and her mom, sister, and I drove to East Oakland.

We pulled up to my mom's apartment and I saw the paramedic's vehicle with their lights on. We parked the car, got out, and started walking toward the apartment. We walked up the stairs and to the front door. It was wide open. My youngest brother was standing beside it. He had his hands in his pockets and his head hung low. I hugged him and tried to comfort him.

I slowly walked into the apartment, down the hall, and into my mom's room. I saw her lying on the floor with her favorite red blanket placed on top of her. I fell to my knees beside her and put my head on her chest. I cried and said "Please get up. This has to be a dream. This can't be real. Please get up Mama. I don't want to lose you. I can't lose you. Please get up." But it was real. It wasn't a dream. Then I said, "I'm sorry. I am so, so sorry."

The morticians came and picked up my mom. They put her in a body bag, placed her on a stretcher, and rolled her out of the apartment. I sat on her bed, and I kept thinking it wasn't real. It had to be a dream.

She couldn't be gone just like that. This doesn't make sense.

Then I felt so much guilt come over me. I shouldn't have lied and told her I already had plans to go out of town. I should have gone back home to spend time with her. She must've needed me. I should have gone home, but I wanted to hang out with my girlfriend. I chose to spend time with her instead of my mom and I was so angry with myself.

After a few minutes, I told my brother I was about to leave. I told him I was going back to my girlfriend's house and I asked him to come with me, but he didn't want to go. So, I told him I would be back in the morning. I got in the car with my girlfriend and her family, and we drove back to North Oakland.

The next day I woke up early, got myself and my son ready, and headed back to my mom's apartment. My cousins and Anne came over. We all started drinking and reminiscing about my mom. We cried and laughed together as we talked about our memories of her.

Anne said my mom was not herself that day. She was incredibly happy. She was singing and dancing. She was even giving away money and pain pills. She said she saw my mom nod off a few times, but she did not think anything of it.

My sister and I thought Anne's story

was odd. We were trying to make sense of her death. And then my youngest brother said it was true. He said, "Mama was acting weird that day. She came into his room that night dancing and singing. She gave me a hug and a kiss before going back into her room. I guess that was her way of saying goodbye. A few hours later I walked into her room to check on her and she wasn't breathing."

We questioned if she accidentally overdosed or if she committed suicide. My mom took pain pills because she had a broken ankle that never healed and she had gangrene in her leg. She was in a lot of pain so, maybe she did accidentally overdose.

My cousins and Anne started to blame

me for my mom's death. They said all she wanted was to spend time with me and her grandson. They said my mom died of a broken heart. She committed suicide because deep down she was sad and lonely.

My girlfriend started defending me and my older cousin got upset. She wanted to fight so she started punching my girlfriend while my girlfriend was holding my son. I grabbed my son out of my girlfriend's arms and told my cousin and Anne to leave. They left my mom's apartment after the fight.

The next day my sister told me my mom apologized to her for all the bad things she said and did. My sister said when she was pregnant with her first child, my mom called her into her room. My mom told my sister she had visited a psychiatrist and she told the psychiatrist she did not want to have another child after she gave birth to me. She wanted to get an abortion when she was pregnant with my sister, but my dad wanted her to keep my sister, so she did. She said she did not feel any emotional connection with my sister during her pregnancy.

The psychiatrist told my mom instead of showing resentment toward my dad for making her keep the baby, she displayed it toward my sister. My mom apologized to my sister, and she said from that day on she was going to be a better mom to her. My sister and I are both grateful that we had an opportunity to forgive my mom before she died.

I planned my mom's memorial with some help. My papa and I paid for her cremation and we had her memorial at 13th Ave Church of Christ. My girlfriend's cousin made the obituary, bought some flowers, and paid for my mom's photo canvas. I bought the food and cooked it too.

A few family members and friends attended my mom's memorial. I told my cousins and Anne they were not invited. My son, siblings, girlfriend, and I sat together in the front row. My sister and I went up to the mic to speak but we could barely talk. We mostly cried.

Our uncle spoke about my mom, and he said she was mean. Everyone started to laugh because it was true. He said she did not sugarcoat anything. She was very blunt and honest. She told it like it was. But she was also very caring. She was willing to help those in need, especially with a place to stay or food to eat. My youngest cousin sang I Will Always Love You by Whitney Houston. We all cried as we listened.

Later that night I started to drink, and I consumed some pain pills I found on my mom's dresser. I took a knife from the kitchen and walked into the bathroom. I sat on the toilet and contemplated cutting my wrist. I kept telling myself I wanted to see her again. I wanted to see my mom and tell her how sorry I was. As I cried and tried to build the courage to take my life, my son started knocking on the bathroom door. He was yelling, "Mama!".

I thought, how could I take my life? How could I leave my son to be in the same predicament I was in? I did not want him to feel the pain I felt. I did not want to transfer my misery over to him. So, I decided to live. I decided to live for him. I opened the door, looked into his eyes, picked him up, and held him tightly. He saved my life.

To this day I want to believe my mom died of an accidental overdose. It's hard to believe she committed suicide. Every time I tried to commit suicide, she always said, " I would never try to take my beautiful life. I look too good to take my life.". But I do not know how she was truly feeling at that moment or what she was thinking at that time.

My siblings and I still try to make sense of her death. She But death doesn't make sense. We all die one day and we don't know when it will happen. All I can do is hope that she is in heaven and that one day I will see her again.

If you are contemplating suicide, please do not do it. You will not end your pain and suffering. You will only transfer that pain and suffering to those who love you. Seek help and trust in God. Ask God for guidance. I believe He will get you through the depression and anxiety, through the hard times and misery. In the future, you will look back and be so grateful and proud of yourself.

It took me a while, but I finally made some positive changes. I finally started working on my spiritual, mental, and physical health. I love who I am, and I love who I'm becoming. I learned from my bad decisions and mistakes. I forgave myself and others. And I am sharing my story to help others who are going through the same things I went through. Things are okay and they will get better.

~Believe, Have Faith, and Manifest~